What Colour is an Orange?

Tristan Boyer Binns

www.raintreepublishers.co.uk
Visit our website to find out more information about **Raintree** books.

To order:
 Phone 44 (0) 1865 888112
 Send a fax to 44 (0) 1865 314091
📠 Visit the Raintree Bookshop at **www.raintreepublishers.co.uk** to browse our catalogue and order online

First published in Great Britain by Raintree, Halley Court, Jordan Hill, Oxford OX2 8EJ, part of Harcourt Education.
Raintree is a registered trademark of Harcourt Education Ltd.

Editorial: Nancy Dickmann and Harriet Milles
Design: Michelle Lisseter and Bigtop
Illustrations: Darren Lingard
Picture Research: Mica Brancic and Maria Joannou
Production: Camilla Smith

Originated by Modern Age
Printed and bound by WKT Company Limited

10-digit ISBN 1 406 20468 4 (hardback)
13-digit ISBN 978-1-4062-0468-1
11 10 09 08 07
10 9 8 7 6 5 4 3 2 1

10-digit ISBN 1 406 20493 5 (paperback)
13-digit ISBN 978-1-4062-0493-3
11 10 09 08 07
10 9 8 7 6 5 4 3 2 1

British Library Cataloguing in Publication Data
Boyer Binns, Tristan
What colour is an orange? – (Fusion)
535.6
A full catalogue record for this book is available from the British Library.

Acknowledgements
The author and publisher are grateful to the following for permission to reproduce copyright material: Alamy **pp. 7** (K-Photos), **21** (Picture Contact); Corbis **pp. 9**, **29** (top) (Zefa/B. Glanzmann), **17** (Ralf-Finn Hestoft), **23** (Torleif Svensson), **25**, **29** (bottom) (Alan Towse/Ecoscene); Getty Images/The Image Bank **pp. 4**, **5**, **28** (top) (Frans Lemmens), **15** (Stephen Cooper); Getty Images/National Geographic **p. 16**; Harcourt Education Limited/Tudor Photography **pp. 13**, **19** (top and bottom), **25**, **27** (top and bottom), **28** (bottom).

Cover photograph of an orange reproduced with permission of Photolibrary.com/Foodpix.

The publishers would like to thank Nancy Harris and Harold Pratt for their assistance in the preparation of this book.

Every effort has been made to contact copyright holders of any material reproduced in this book. Any omissions will be rectified in subsequent printings if notice is given to the publishers.

Disclaimer
All the Internet addresses (URLs) given in this book were valid at the time of going to press. However, due to the dynamic nature of the Internet, some addresses may have changed, or sites may have changed or ceased to exist since publication. While the author and publishers regret any inconvenience this may cause readers, no responsibility for any such changes can be accepted by either the author or the publishers.

It is recommended that adults supervise children on the Internet.

Contents

Some words are printed in bold, **like this**. You can find out what they mean on page 30. You can also look in the box at the bottom of the page where they first appear.

No light, no orange

An orange is orange, right? Of course it is! But that is not the whole story. How do you see the colour orange? Why is the orange that colour? Why is it not red or blue? Let's follow the story of colour to find out.

You need light to see. You need light to see colour. Look at the first picture. At sunrise, there is very little light. All the colours in the world look grey. Why is that?

▼ *Before the Sun comes up the colours in the market are very dull.*

We can only see colours when light is strong. When the Sun rises, the light fills the sky. All the colours seem to wake up in sunlight. Look at the second picture. The sunlight is strong. Now the oranges and apples look bright!

▼ *The Sun comes up. Now the colours pop out at you.*

5

Splitting light

Look at the sunlight. It does not seem to have any colour. We call it **white light**. White light is really made up of all the different colours. Sometimes you can see these colours.

Light bends when it travels from air to glass. This is called **refraction**. A **prism** is a solid glass triangle. If you shine white light on to a prism, the light bends.

Each colour of light bends a little more than the colour next to it. Light splits when it leaves the prism. It splits up into all its different colours. You see a band of bright colours. This band of colours is called the **spectrum**.

prism	solid glass triangle that splits up white light into its colours
refraction	way that light bends when it moves from one see-through material to another
spectrum	colours that white light splits into
white light	light made up of all the colours mixed together

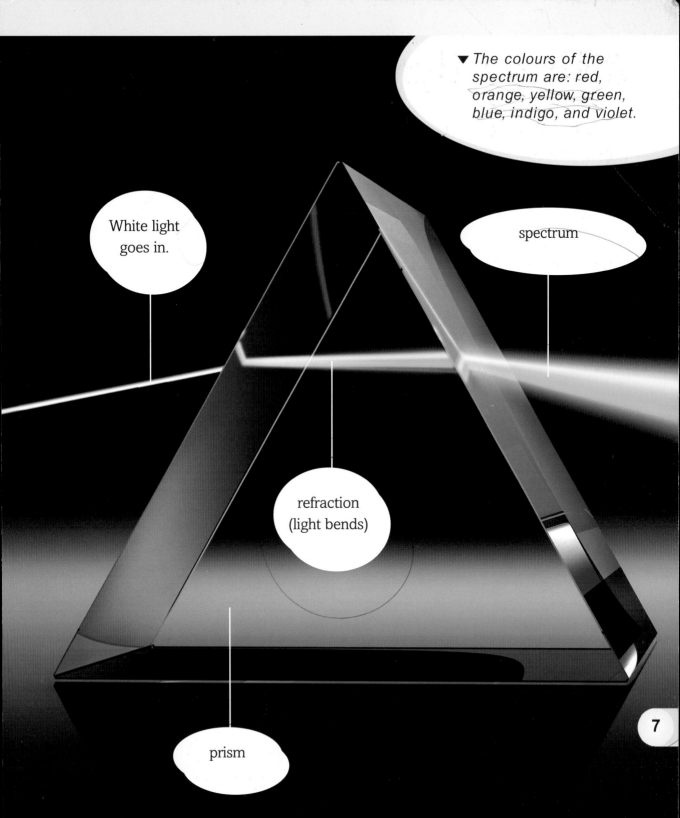

▼ The colours of the spectrum are: red, orange, yellow, green, blue, indigo, and violet.

White light goes in.

spectrum

refraction (light bends)

prism

I can see a rainbow

Do the **spectrum** colours look familiar? A rainbow is a spectrum. Sometimes when it rains, sunlight hits the raindrops. The raindrops act as **prisms**. Each raindrop **refracts** (bends) the **white light** from the Sun. A band of colours comes out of each raindrop. Together they make a rainbow.

You can also make white light out of coloured light. Put a curved glass **lens** between two prisms. Shine white light on the first prism. The spectrum will pass through the glass lens. All the colours bend back in the second prism. They mix together again. The light comes back out of the second prism as white light.

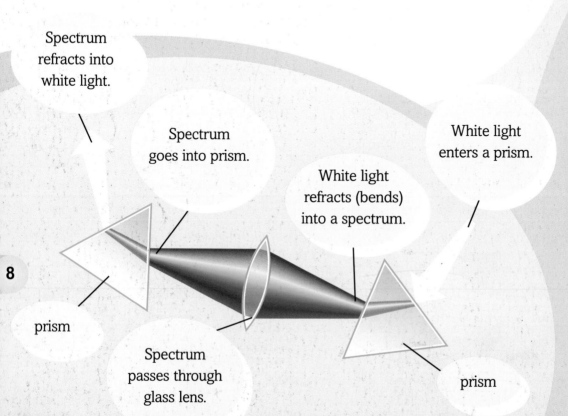

Spectrum refracts into white light.

Spectrum goes into prism.

White light refracts (bends) into a spectrum.

White light enters a prism.

prism

Spectrum passes through glass lens.

prism

8

▼ *A rainbow shows you the whole spectrum of colours.*

Splitting light

Sir Isaac Newton was a scientist. He was the first person to do the prism experiment. He did it almost 350 years ago. He showed how light split into colours. Then he mixed the colours back into white light.

lens piece of glass curved on one or both sides

Trapping light

Your eyes and your brain work together to see colour. Light goes into your eye. It hits the **retina** at the back of the eye. The retina picks up light. Inside the retina are special parts called **cones**.

There are three kinds of cone. One cone senses only red light. One cone senses only green light. One cone senses only blue light.

The cones tell your brain what they have seen. Imagine you are looking at **white light**. There are no cones to see white. The red cones send a message to your brain. They say they have seen the red part of the white light. The green cones say they have seen the green part. The blue cones say they have seen the blue part.

Then your brain mixes all the colours together. If you mix red, green, and blue light, they make white light. Your brain knows you have seen white light. Amazing!

cones parts of the retina that sense red, blue, and green
retina part of the back of the eye that picks up light

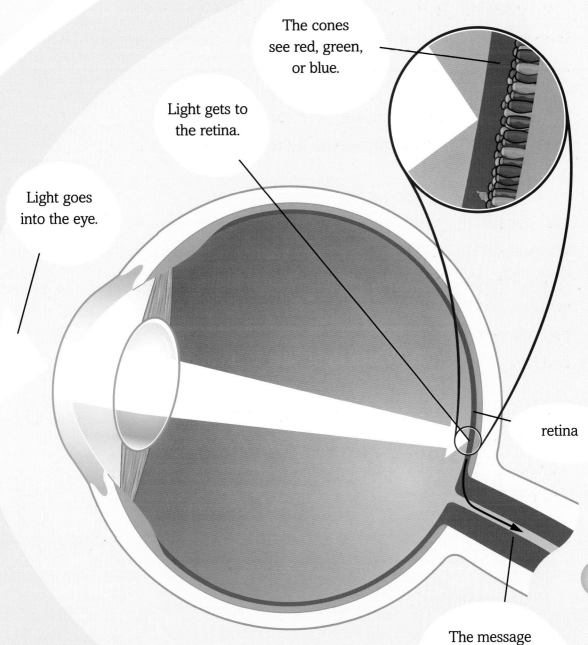

▼ *This diagram shows how the eye sees colour.*

The cones see red, green, or blue.

Light gets to the retina.

Light goes into the eye.

retina

The message about the colours goes to the brain.

Seeing orange

A **light source** gives off its own light. The Sun is a light source. Light bulbs are also light sources. Light from a light source comes straight into your eyes. It does not bounce off anything else. You see it as white or coloured light.

Most things around us are not light sources. They do not give off their own light the way the Sun does.

Think of the orange. Light falls on it from a light source. For example, the Sun might shine on it. The light bounces back off the orange. It bounces into your eyes. This is called **reflected** light. We see most things in the world with reflected light.

Here is the clever bit. **White light** falls on an orange. The orange reflects back only the orange light. It traps, or **absorbs**, all the other colours in the white light. The reflected orange light goes into your eyes. You see orange!

absorb	trap or soak up
light source	something that gives off its own light
reflect	bounce back

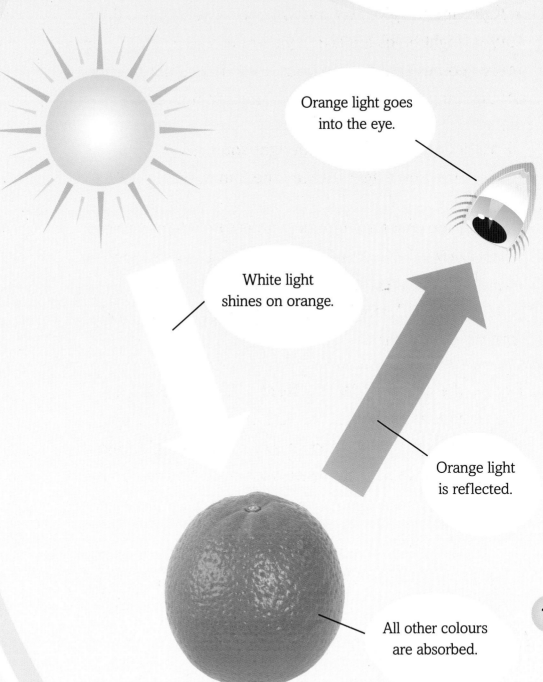

▼ *This is how you see an orange.*

Orange light goes into the eye.

White light shines on orange.

Orange light is reflected.

All other colours are absorbed.

13

Colour kings

Have you ever seen a black-and-white film? There is no colour, but you can still see light and dark. There are details and shadows.

Think of a football match. Without colour it would be hard to tell the teams apart. People use colour to tell things apart that have the same shapes.

Colours can also make people feel things. Blue can make you feel calm. Orange can make you feel like jumping around.

Colour cones

Cones are part of your eyes. They let you see colour. Some people have red and green cones in their eyes that do not do their jobs properly. They cannot tell between red and green. This is called being **colour blind**.

Cats and dogs have very few cones in their eyes. The ones they have are weak. They only see faded colours.

colour blind   not being able to tell between different colours

Most people see the world in bright colour.

Cats and dogs cannot see much colour.

15

A world without colour would be black, white, and grey.

Just licking a ▼ poison-dart frog will make most animals very sick. It is brightly coloured. This is to warn animals that it has poisonous skin.

16

poison Something that causes sickness or death

Watch out!

Bright colours make us look. They catch our eyes. This makes them very good for warnings.

Many small animals are food for bigger animals. They need ways to stop being eaten. Some small animals have **poison** in their bodies. Others taste bad. These small animals are brightly coloured. The colours say, "watch out!" A bigger animal may eat one and get sick. Next time it sees the same colours it will know to stay away!

Road signs are bright yellow or red. They can warn drivers about dangers ahead. Red and white lights on bicycles show drivers where they are. Ambulances have bright paint and flashing lights. They warn us to get out of their way.

Workers on an ▶ airport runway wear bright vests. They need to show aircraft pilots where they are.

Back to basics

What makes red, yellow, and blue special? They are **primary colours**. These three colours can be mixed to make all the other colours. You mix different amounts to get different colours.

Colours for print

Red, yellow, and blue are the primary colours of paint. There are other primary colours. Cyan, magenta, and yellow are also primary colours. Printers use them to print books. This book was printed using cyan, magenta, and yellow ink.

▼ *The set on the left are the primary colours of paint. The set on the right are the primary colours that printers use.*

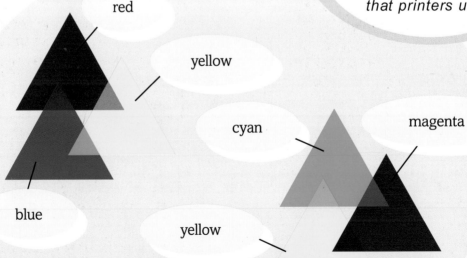

red

yellow

cyan

magenta

blue

yellow

primary colours   set of three colours that can be mixed to make all the other colours

You can mix red and yellow paint to make orange. You can mix yellow and blue paint to make green. But no matter how many colours you mix together, you can never make red, yellow, or blue.

◀ *If you mix the same colours in different amounts you get different results. Mix the same amount of yellow and blue. You get a strong green.*

▼*Mix more yellow with less blue. You get a yellowy green.*

Mixing paint

Paint is not a **light source**. You can only see paint colours when light shines on them. The light can come from the Sun. It can come from a light bulb.

You see paint colours because of the way they **absorb** (trap) and **reflect** (bounce off) light. Think of a blue car. The blue paint absorbs all colours in the **spectrum** except blue. Blue is the only colour left. The other colours have been trapped. Only the blue light reflects off the car into your eyes.

When you mix paint colours they can get darker. This is because each paint colour absorbs light. When they are mixed together they absorb a lot of light.

Think of a set of paints. Mix together the three **primary colours** of red, yellow, and blue. They absorb so much light that they make black.

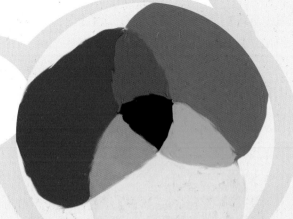

You can make every▶ colour except white by mixing the primary colours of paint.

20

▼ The paint colours on this boy's face absorb and reflect light.

Adding lights

Think back to the **prism**. A prism is a solid triangle.
It splits **white light** into all the colours. If you mix all
the coloured lights back together you get white light again.

The **primary colours** of light are red, green, and blue.
You can mix them to make all of the other colours of light.
When you mix them, you add their light together. If you
mix all three primary colours of paint, you get black. But
mixing all three primary colours of light makes white light.

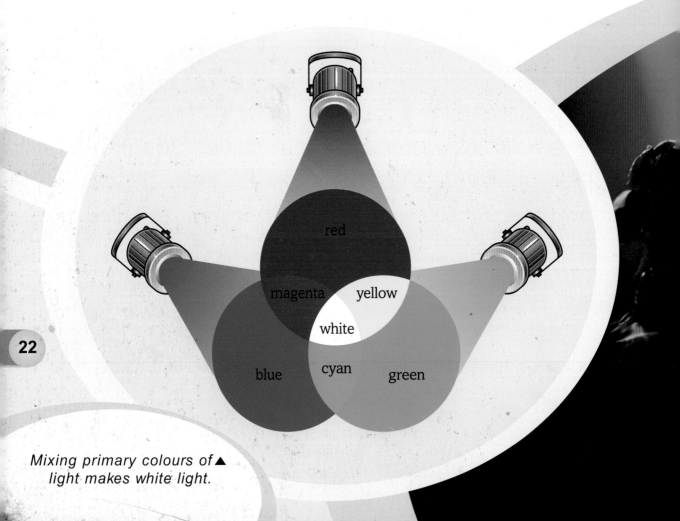

*Mixing primary colours of ▲
light makes white light.*

The **cones** in your eyes can see only the colours red, green, and blue. So how do you see all of the other colours? It's easy! You see the primary colours of light.

Look at something yellow. Your red and green cones send signals to your brain. Your brain mixes the red and green signals. It knows you have seen yellow.

▼ *People mix coloured lights for dances and shows.*

Hey! My orange is on TV!

Guess how many colours are on your television screen? Only three! Your TV screen is just groups of three tiny colour dots.

These dots glow red, green, or blue. They glow the **primary colours** of light. The three colours can be mixed to make every other colour. They also make white. This is how you see all the colours on your TV.

A group that makes up a red part of the picture will only glow red. A group that makes up an orange part will glow red and green. The **cones** in your eyes see the red and green light. Your brain mixes the glowing dots to see orange.

TV colours

A TV camera points at an orange. It takes a picture of it. The picture is broken into tiny dots. For every point on the orange there are three dots. There is one for red, one for green, and one for blue. Each dot is turned into a signal. The signals are sent. Your TV at home gets the signals. These signals tell each dot in the group of three how to glow.

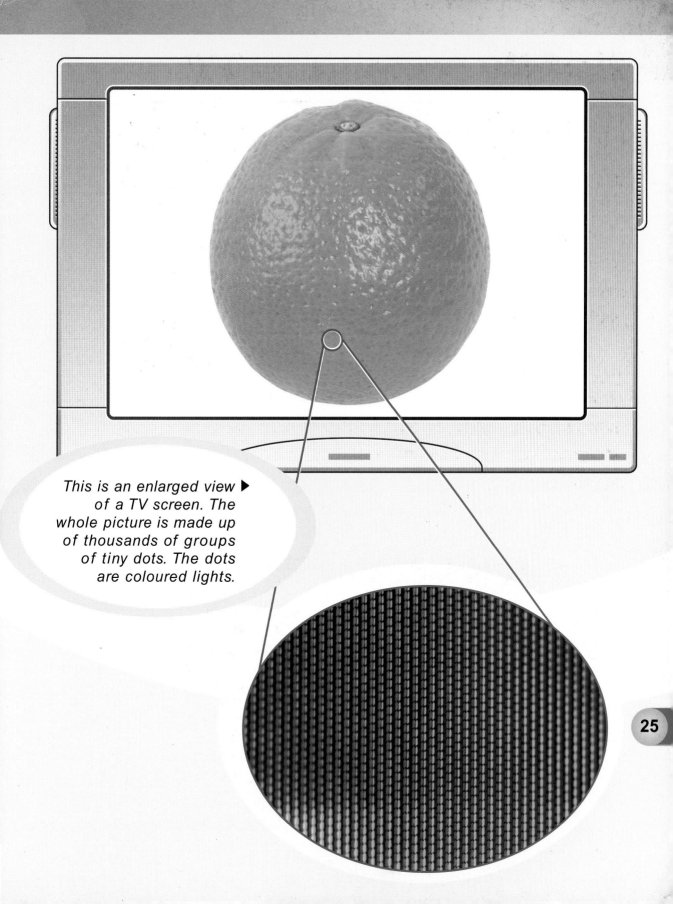

This is an enlarged view ▶ of a TV screen. The whole picture is made up of thousands of groups of tiny dots. The dots are coloured lights.

Hey! My orange is black!

You can do some good tricks with coloured light.

What happens when the light that shines on to an orange is not **white light**? Does the orange still **absorb** (soak up) light? Does it still **reflect** (bounce back) light in the same way? If you shine blue light on to an orange, is it still orange? No!

Shine a blue light on your orange. Orange light is made up of red and green light. The blue light has had its red and green light taken out. The orange has no red or green to reflect. It looks black!

Have a look at the football. Most of it is white. It reflects all the colours that shine on it. It absorbs none. What happens when the only colour that shines on it is blue? It only has blue to reflect, so it looks blue! What else can you use your colour tricks on?

◀ You can do this colour trick by taping a piece of see-through blue plastic on the front of a torch. The white light will shine blue through the plastic.

Colour diary

Now you know how light and colour work. It's all in the way you see it!

Monday

Bought oranges at the market. They were soaking up blue light. They were **reflecting** red and green light. Guess what? They looked orange!

Tuesday

Mixed paints. Made green from blue and yellow paint.

Wednesday
Saw a rainbow. Cool colours!

Thursday
Made my own rainbow!
Shone a torch through a
prism. Watched the white
light split into colours.

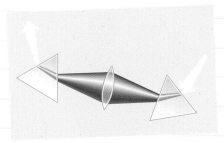

Friday
Wore my orange T-shirt to the school disco.
It looked black in the blue lights.

Saturday
Watched football on TV. Can't
believe it was just a mass of red,
green, and blue dots. Weird!

Sunday
Stayed in bed late.
No colour to be seen.

Glossary

absorb trap or soak up. A sponge absorbs spilled juice.

colour blind not being able to tell between different colours.

cones parts of the retina that sense red, blue, and green. The cones in your eyes see colours.

lens piece of glass curved on one or both sides

light source something that gives off its own light. The Sun, a torch, and a candle are all light sources.

poison something that causes sickness or death. Strong poison from some snake bites can kill people.

primary colours set of three colours that can be mixed to make all the other colours. Primary colours are bright.

prism solid glass triangle that splits up white light into its colours. A prism makes a rainbow of colour.

reflect bounce back. A mirror reflects what is in front of it.

refraction way that light bends when it moves from one see-through material to another. A straw looks like it is bending in a glass of water because of refraction.

retina part of the back of the eye that picks up light. You see pictures on your retina.

spectrum colours that white light splits into. They are: red, orange, yellow, green, blue, indigo, and violet. The spectrum is easy to see in the colours of the rainbow.

white light light made up of all the colours mixed together. White light comes from the Sun.